D0290731

THE LITTLE BOOK OF
GRAND
PARENTING

FREDDIE GREEN

summersdale

TO..........................

FROM........................

THE IDEA THAT NO ONE
IS PERFECT IS A VIEW
MOST COMMONLY
HELD BY PEOPLE WITH
NO GRANDCHILDREN.

Doug Larson

THEY SAY GENES
SKIP GENERATIONS.
MAYBE THAT'S WHY
GRANDPARENTS FIND
THEIR GRANDCHILDREN
SO LIKEABLE.

Joan McIntosh

YOU HAVE LOCKS
ON ALL YOUR
CUPBOARDS - WHICH
IS A NIGHTMARE
WHEN YOU NEED AN
URGENT TONIC (NOT
TO MENTION A GIN).

WHEN GRANDPARENTS ENTER THE DOOR, DISCIPLINE FLIES OUT THE WINDOW.

Ogden Nash

NOBODY CAN DO FOR
LITTLE CHILDREN WHAT
GRANDPARENTS DO.
GRANDPARENTS SORT
OF SPRINKLE STARDUST
OVER THE LIVES OF
LITTLE CHILDREN.

Alex Haley

YOU REALISE THAT
SNAILS AREN'T THE
ONLY CREATURES
THAT LEAVE A
TRAIL OF GOO
BEHIND THEM.

ONE OF THE MOST
POWERFUL HANDCLASPS
IS THAT OF A NEW
GRANDBABY AROUND
THE FINGER OF
A GRANDFATHER.

Joy Hargrove

YOU REALISE THAT
YOU ARE NOW
THE HEAD OF AN
ONGOING DYNASTY.

**YOUR HOUSE
HAS GONE
FROM SPOTLESS
TO SHAMELESS.**

**WHEN YOU HAVE A
GRANDCHILD, YOU
HAVE TWO CHILDREN.**

Jewish proverb

WE FIND DELIGHT IN THE
BEAUTY AND HAPPINESS
OF CHILDREN THAT
MAKES THE HEART TOO
BIG FOR THE BODY.

Ralph Waldo Emerson

YOUR MANTELPIECE
IS OVERFLOWING
WITH PHOTOS OF
YOUR GRANDKIDS'
MILESTONES AND
ACHIEVEMENTS.

YOU HAVE A BIG
TIN OF SWEETS
ON PERMANENT
STANDBY –
ANY EXCUSE!

FAMILY MEANS PUTTING YOUR ARMS AROUND EACH OTHER AND BEING THERE.

Barbara Bush

YOU ARE THE SUN, GRANDMA, YOU ARE THE SUN IN MY LIFE.

Kitty Tsui

EVERYONE IS THE AGE OF THEIR HEART.

Guatemalan proverb

ON BABYSITTING
DAYS, YOU START
HITTING THE
BOTTLE AT 4 P.M.
INSTEAD OF 7 P.M.

SOME OF THE
WORLD'S BEST EDUCATORS
ARE GRANDPARENTS.

Charles W. Shedd

HAVE CHILDREN WHILE YOUR PARENTS ARE STILL YOUNG ENOUGH TO TAKE CARE OF THEM.

Rita Rudner

**YOU RELEARN HOW
TO MAKE COINS
MAGICALLY APPEAR
FROM BEHIND
CHILDREN'S EARS.**

THOSE WHO HAVE NO GRANDPARENTS LOSE VERY MUCH.

Spanish proverb

THERE ARE RUBBER
DUCKS ON THE SIDE
OF THE BATH AGAIN –
AND SOMETIMES YOU
EVEN LET THE KIDS
PLAY WITH THEM.

YOU FIND YOURSELF
SINGING 'ROW, ROW,
ROW YOUR BOAT'
AT INAPPROPRIATE
MOMENTS.

IF GRANDMAS HADN'T EXISTED, KIDS WOULD HAVE INEVITABLY INVENTED THEM.

Arthur Kornhaber

A GRANDFATHER IS
SOMEONE YOU CAN
LOOK UP TO NO MATTER
HOW TALL YOU GROW.

Anonymous

THE GRANDCHILDREN
SEEM TO BE OFF
TO SCHOOL FIVE
MINUTES AFTER
THEY'VE BEEN BORN.

YOUR BAKING NOW
INVOLVES HUNDREDS
AND THOUSANDS
OR RICE KRISPIES.

FAMILY IS THE MOST
IMPORTANT THING
IN THE WORLD.

Diana, Princess of Wales

**NEVER HAVE CHILDREN,
ONLY GRANDCHILDREN.**

Gore Vidal

A GRANDAM'S NAME IS
LITTLE LESS IN LOVE
THAN IS THE DOTING
TITLE OF A MOTHER.

William Shakespeare

YOU HAVE
EVEN MORE GREY
HAIR THAN YOU
USED TO.

THE ONLY ROCK I KNOW
THAT STAYS STEADY,
THE ONLY INSTITUTION
I KNOW THAT WORKS,
IS THE FAMILY.

Lee Iacocca

THERE'S NO PLACE LIKE HOME... EXCEPT GRANDMA'S.

Anonymous

YOU HAVE A GO
ON THE PARK'S
SWINGS FOR THE
FIRST TIME IN
YEARS – WHOOPEE!

MY GRANDMOTHER IS
OVER 80 AND STILL
DOESN'T NEED GLASSES.
DRINKS RIGHT OUT
OF THE BOTTLE.

Henny Youngman

YOUR IDEA
OF A GOOD TIME
IS GOING TO
THE ZOO.

YOU HAVE
YOUR VERY OWN
BUCKET AND SPADE
ONCE MORE.

CHILDREN WILL NOT
REMEMBER YOU FOR
THE MATERIAL THINGS
YOU PROVIDED, BUT
FOR THE FEELING THAT
YOU CHERISHED THEM.

Richard L. Evans

NO COWBOY WAS EVER FASTER ON THE DRAW THAN A GRANDPARENT PULLING A BABY PICTURE OUT OF A WALLET.

Anonymous

DESPITE YOUR
RELATIVE YOUTH,
YOU SUDDENLY
FEEL VERY ANCIENT
BEING CALLED
'GRAND' ANYTHING.

YOUR AFTERNOON
NAPS ARE NOW
INTERRUPTED BY
BEING KICKED
IN THE SHINS.

FAMILY FACES ARE
MAGIC MIRRORS. LOOKING
AT PEOPLE WHO BELONG
TO US, WE SEE THE PAST,
PRESENT AND FUTURE.

Gail Lumet Buckley

FEW THINGS ARE MORE
DELIGHTFUL THAN
GRANDCHILDREN
FIGHTING OVER
YOUR LAP.

Doug Larson

GRANDCHILDREN ARE THE
DOTS THAT CONNECT THE
LINES FROM GENERATION
TO GENERATION.

Lois Wyse

HALF YOUR
CHRISTMAS
SHOPPING IS NOW
DONE IN A TOYSHOP.

GRANDFATHERS ARE FOR LOVING AND FIXING THINGS.

Anonymous

GROWING OLD IS MANDATORY; GROWING UP IS OPTIONAL.

Chili Davis

**YOU ONLY CHECK
THE TV GUIDE
UP TO 6 P.M. ON
BABYSITTING DAYS.**

IT IS AS GRANDMOTHERS
THAT OUR MOTHERS
COME INTO THE FULLNESS
OF THEIR GRACE.

Christopher Morley

YOUR OTHER HALF ISN'T THE ONLY ONE DRIBBLING AND TALKING NONSENSE.

YOU'VE GOT HEAD
LICE FOR THE
FIRST TIME SINCE
LEAVING SCHOOL.

GRANDPARENTS,
LIKE HEROES, ARE AS
NECESSARY TO A CHILD'S
GROWTH AS VITAMINS.

Joyce Allston

THERE IS NO CURE FOR LAZINESS BUT A LARGE FAMILY HELPS.

Herbert V. Prochnow

THERE ARE
UNIDENTIFIABLE
STICKY PATCHES ON
YOUR CAR SEATS.

YOU ENCOURAGE
THE KIDS TO EAT
THEIR GREENS
EVEN THOUGH YOU
HAVEN'T A CLUE
WHAT KALE OR
SAMPHIRE ARE.

**BEING GRANDPARENTS
SUFFICIENTLY
REMOVES US FROM THE
RESPONSIBILITIES SO THAT
WE CAN BE FRIENDS.**

Allan Frome

YOU HAVE TO DO YOUR OWN GROWING, NO MATTER HOW TALL YOUR GRANDFATHER WAS.

Anonymous

**LEARNING IS EVER
IN THE FRESHNESS
OF ITS YOUTH,
EVEN FOR THE OLD.**

Aeschylus

YOU'RE BABYSITTING AGAIN – BUT NOT GETTING PAID FOR IT!

IT'S IMPOSSIBLE FOR
A GRANDMOTHER TO
UNDERSTAND THAT FEW
PEOPLE... WILL FIND
HER GRANDCHILD AS
ENDEARING AS SHE DOES.

Janet Lanese

THE HAPPIEST MOMENTS
OF MY LIFE HAVE BEEN
THE FEW WHICH I HAVE
PASSED AT HOME IN THE
BOSOM OF MY FAMILY.

Thomas Jefferson

YOU'RE
ENCOURAGED TO
TALK ABOUT 'THE
OLDEN DAYS' I.E.
YOUR YOUTH!

ON THE SEVENTH
DAY GOD RESTED. HIS
GRANDCHILDREN MUST
HAVE BEEN OUT OF TOWN.

Gene Perret

THERE'S A STRANGE
CRUNCHING
SOUND THESE DAYS
WHEN YOU WALK
ACROSS THE LIVING
ROOM CARPET.

YOUR LIVING
ROOM HAS BEEN
TRANSFORMED
INTO A HAZARDOUS
ASSAULT COURSE
BECAUSE IT'S
LITTERED WITH
TOYS, BANANA SKINS
AND NAPPIES.

BECOMING A
GRANDMOTHER IS
WONDERFUL. ONE MOMENT
YOU'RE JUST A MOTHER.
THE NEXT YOU ARE ALL-
WISE AND PREHISTORIC.

Pam Brown

BLESSED BE THE TIES THAT BIND GENERATIONS.

Anonymous

YOU HAVE TO
DIG THAT OLD
HIGH CHAIR OUT
OF THE LOFT.

YOU NOW HAVE A
VERY SMALL CHILD
SHOWING YOU HOW
TO USE YOUR PHONE.

IN TIME OF TEST, FAMILY IS BEST.

Burmese proverb

A GRANDMOTHER
PRETENDS SHE DOESN'T
KNOW WHO YOU ARE
ON HALLOWEEN.

Erma Bombeck

THERE IS NO GRANDFATHER WHO DOES NOT ADORE HIS GRANDSON.

Victor Hugo

YOU ENTER A
STRANGE NEW
WORLD OF FOOD
OPTIONS – POTATOES
NOW HAVE SMILEY
FACES INSTEAD
OF JUST EYES.

TWO THINGS I
DISLIKE ABOUT MY
GRANDDAUGHTER:
WHEN SHE WON'T TAKE
HER AFTERNOON NAP,
AND WHEN SHE WON'T
LET ME TAKE MINE.

Gene Perret

IF YOU KNOW
HIS FATHER AND
GRANDFATHER, DON'T
WORRY ABOUT HIS SON.

Moroccan proverb

YOU REALISE WHY
YOUR KIDS ARE SO
KEEN TO PASS THEIR
KIDS OVER TO YOU
FOR THE DAY!

THE FAMILY
IS ONE OF NATURE'S
MASTERPIECES.

George Santayana

YOU HAVE
BECOME A HYBRID
OF STAND-UP
COMEDIAN,
MAGICIAN, CHEF
AND NURSE.

YOU DISCOVER THAT ALL THE BEDTIME STORIES THAT YOU REMEMBER ARE A BIT POLITICALLY INCORRECT THESE DAYS.

**THE SIMPLEST TOY,
ONE WHICH EVEN THE
YOUNGEST CHILD CAN
OPERATE, IS CALLED
A GRANDPARENT.**

Sam Levenson

WRINKLES SHOULD MERELY INDICATE WHERE SMILES HAVE BEEN.

Mark Twain

YOU REALISE THAT
EVERYTHING YOU
LEARNED ABOUT
BABIES ALL THOSE
YEARS AGO HAS
BEEN COMPLETELY
FORGOTTEN.

YOU FIND THAT
SWINGING CHILDREN
AROUND, LIKE YOU
USED TO WITH
YOUR OWN, PUTS
YOUR BACK OUT
FOR A FORTNIGHT.

YOU DO NOT
REALLY UNDERSTAND
SOMETHING UNLESS
YOU CAN EXPLAIN IT TO
YOUR GRANDMOTHER.

Proverb

YOU DON'T CHOOSE YOUR FAMILY. THEY ARE GOD'S GIFT TO YOU, AS YOU ARE TO THEM.

Desmond Tutu

IN ORDER TO INFLUENCE
A CHILD, ONE MUST BE
CAREFUL NOT TO BE
THAT CHILD'S PARENT
OR GRANDPARENT.

Don Marquis

YOU DISCOVER THAT
THE PRICE OF KIDS'
ICE LOLLIES HAS
TRIPLED SINCE YOU
LAST BOUGHT ONE.

THE OLD ARE THE
PRECIOUS GEM
IN THE CENTRE OF
THE HOUSEHOLD.

Chinese proverb

ELEPHANTS AND GRANDCHILDREN NEVER FORGET.

Andy Rooney

YOUR STAIRCASE
HAS A SAFETY
GATE – WHICH
YOU UNWISELY
TRY TO CLIMB
OVER WITHOUT
UNLOCKING IT.

THE BEST BABYSITTERS ARE, OF COURSE, THE BABY'S GRANDPARENTS.

Dave Barry

YOU'RE DELIGHTED
THAT BABIES NEED
AFTERNOON NAPS
- AND YOU LEARN
TO COORDINATE
YOURS WITH THEIRS.

**YOU REDISCOVER
THE MAGIC OF
CHRISTMAS AND
GET QUITE CLOSE
TO WRITING TO
SANTA YOURSELF.**

THE BABY IS NOT YET BORN, AND YET YOU SAY THAT HIS NOSE IS LIKE HIS GRANDFATHER'S.

Indian proverb

A GRANDMOTHER IS A
MOTHER WHO HAS A
SECOND CHANCE.

Anonymous

ON RECEIVING A
LETTER ADDRESSED
'DEAR GRANDMA/
GRANDAD', YOU'RE
QUITE SHOCKED
TO REALISE IT
MEANS YOU!

YOU CAN NO LONGER
KEEP ANYTHING
SAFELY ON THE
LOW SHELVES –
UNFORTUNATELY
THESE ARE THE ONES
YOU CAN REACH
MOST COMFORTABLY.

PERHAPS THE GREATEST
SOCIAL SERVICE THAT
CAN BE RENDERED BY
ANYBODY... TO MANKIND
IS TO BRING UP A FAMILY.

George Bernard Shaw

THE SOUL IS HEALED BY BEING WITH CHILDREN.

Fyodor Dostoyevsky

A GRANDMOTHER IS A
LITTLE BIT PARENT, A
LITTLE BIT TEACHER AND A
LITTLE BIT BEST FRIEND.

Anonymous

ONE DAY YOU HAVE
TO URGENTLY CHECK
WHETHER YOU'VE HAD
CHICKENPOX ALREADY.

PERFECT LOVE SOMETIMES DOES NOT COME UNTIL THE FIRST GRANDCHILD.

Welsh proverb

IT NOW COSTS MORE
TO AMUSE A CHILD
THAN IT ONCE DID TO
EDUCATE HIS FATHER.

Vaughn Monroe

DURING BABYSITTING DUTY, YOU'RE ASLEEP BEFORE THE GRANDCHILDREN.

GRANDCHILDREN DON'T
MAKE A MAN FEEL OLD;
IT'S THE KNOWLEDGE
THAT HE'S MARRIED TO
A GRANDMOTHER.

J. Norman Collie

YOU FIND IT'S
NOT DÉJÀ VU;
IT'S JUST YOUR
GRANDCHILDREN
GETTING UP TO THE
SAME MISCHIEF AS
THEIR PARENTS.

**YOUR HOUSE BOASTS
A NEW RANGE OF
ALARMING ODOURS.**

EVERYONE NEEDS TO
HAVE ACCESS BOTH TO
GRANDPARENTS AND
GRANDCHILDREN IN
ORDER TO BE A FULL
HUMAN BEING.

Margaret Mead

A GRANDFATHER IS
SOMEONE WITH SILVER
IN HIS HAIR AND GOLD
IN HIS HEART.

Anonymous

YOU BLAME
YOUR 'SENIOR
MOMENTS' ON
YOUR GRANDPARENT
STATUS – EVEN
THOUGH YOU'RE
NOT THAT OLD!

**YOU'RE ABSOLUTELY
SHATTERED BY TEATIME.**

OUR GRANDCHILDREN
ACCEPT US FOR
OURSELVES, WITHOUT
REBUKE OR EFFORT
TO CHANGE US.

Ruth Goode

AN OUNCE OF BLOOD IS
WORTH MORE THAN A
POUND OF FRIENDSHIP.

Spanish proverb

IF I HAD KNOWN HOW
WONDERFUL IT WOULD BE
TO HAVE GRANDCHILDREN,
I'D HAVE HAD THEM FIRST.

Lois Wyse

FOR THE FIRST
TIME IN DECADES,
YOU KNOW WHO
ALL THE LATEST
POP BANDS ARE.

A HOUSE NEEDS A
GRANDMA IN IT.

Louisa May Alcott

**WHEN YOU LOOK AT
YOUR LIFE THE GREATEST
HAPPINESSES ARE
FAMILY HAPPINESSES.**

Joyce Brothers

YOU'RE FLATTERED
IF YOU'RE MISTAKEN
FOR ONE OF THE
PARENTS WHEN
YOU PICK THE
GRANDCHILDREN
UP FROM SCHOOL.

> ## A GRANDMOTHER IS A BABYSITTER WHO WATCHES THE KIDS INSTEAD OF THE TELEVISION.
>
> Anonymous

YOUR IDEA OF
WORKING OUT IS
TRYING TO PICK
UP A GRANDCHILD
FOR A KISS.

YOU LEARN THAT GRANDCHILDREN'S KISSES COME IN TWO SIZES: BIG AND SLOPPY, OR NON-EXISTENT WHEN THEY GET 'TOO OLD' FOR THEM.

ONE OF LIFE'S GREATEST
MYSTERIES IS HOW THE
BOY WHO WASN'T GOOD
ENOUGH TO MARRY
YOUR DAUGHTER CAN
BE THE FATHER OF THE
SMARTEST GRANDCHILD
IN THE WORLD.

Jewish proverb

REJOICE WITH YOUR FAMILY IN THE BEAUTIFUL LAND OF LIFE!

Albert Einstein

YOU DON'T REALISE
HOW QUIET YOUR
HOUSE USED TO
BE UNTIL THE
GRANDCHILDREN
HAVE GONE HOME.

YOU HAVE TO
LOCK THE CAT AWAY
SOMEWHERE FOR ITS
OWN SAFETY WHEN THE
GRANDCHILDREN VISIT.

**IF NOTHING IS
GOING WELL, CALL
YOUR GRANDMOTHER.**

Italian proverb

GRANDPARENTS ARE A
DELIGHTFUL BLEND OF
LAUGHTER, CARING
DEEDS, WONDERFUL
STORIES AND LOVE.

Anonymous

EVERY GENERATION
REVOLTS AGAINST
ITS FATHERS AND
MAKES FRIENDS WITH
ITS GRANDFATHERS.

Lewis Mumford

YOU'RE EXTREMELY
PROUD OF BEING
A GRANDPARENT
THOUGH, FRANKLY,
YOU DIDN'T HAVE
MUCH SAY IN
THE MATTER.

GRANDMOTHER –
A WONDERFUL
MOTHER WITH LOTS
OF PRACTICE.

Anonymous

GRANDCHILDREN
ARE GOD'S WAY OF
COMPENSATING US
FOR GROWING OLD.

Mary H. Waldrip

YOU'RE GIVEN
A LIST OF FOOD
ALLERGIES BEFORE
THE GRANDCHILDREN
CAN COME FOR
A MEAL.

SURELY, TWO OF THE
MOST SATISFYING
EXPERIENCES IN LIFE
MUST BE THOSE OF
BEING A GRANDCHILD
OR A GRANDPARENT.

Donald A. Norberg

NOT FOR THE FIRST
TIME IN YOUR LIFE,
YOU'RE ALMOST
WORD-PERFECT
ON A WHOLE
REPERTOIRE OF
NURSERY RHYMES,
KIDS' SONGS AND
CORNY JOKES.

YOU'RE SHOCKED TO
DISCOVER THAT WATER
PISTOLS THESE DAYS
SEEM TO HAVE THE
FIREPOWER OF AK-47S.

IT SEEMS TO ME THAT
GRANDFATHERS ARE A
LOT YOUNGER THAN
THEY USED TO BE BEFORE
I GOT TO BE ONE.

Andy Rooney

A GRANDPARENT IS OLD ON THE OUTSIDE BUT YOUNG ON THE INSIDE.

Anonymous

YOUR PREVIOUSLY
PRISTINE GARDEN
LOOKS LIKE AN
ADVENTURE
PLAYGROUND AFTER
A HURRICANE.

YOU NEED TO
BRUSH UP YOUR
COMPUTER SKILLS IN
ORDER TO HELP THE
GRANDCHILDREN WITH
THEIR HOMEWORK.

AN HOUR WITH YOUR
GRANDCHILDREN CAN
MAKE YOU FEEL YOUNG
AGAIN. ANYTHING LONGER
THAN THAT, AND YOU
START TO AGE QUICKLY.

Gene Perret

IT IS ONE OF NATURE'S
WAYS THAT WE OFTEN
FEEL CLOSER TO DISTANT
GENERATIONS THAN TO THE
GENERATION IMMEDIATELY
PRECEDING US.

Igor Stravinsky

A MAN'S MATURITY
CONSISTS IN HAVING
FOUND AGAIN THE
SERIOUSNESS ONE HAD
AS A CHILD, AT PLAY.

Friedrich Nietzsche

YOU KNOW YOU'RE A GRANDPARENT WHEN...

YOU REGRET
DONATING ALL
THOSE OLD DISNEY
FILMS TO THE
CHARITY SHOP.

**GRANDMAS ARE
MUMS WITH LOTS
OF ICING.**

Anonymous

IT'S NOT THAT AGE
BRINGS CHILDHOOD
BACK AGAIN. AGE
MERELY SHOWS WHAT
CHILDREN WE REMAIN.

Johann Wolfgang von Goethe

YOUR OWN CHILDREN ARE ASKING FOR ADVICE ON CHILD-REARING AND YOU CAN'T REMEMBER A THING!

THE IMPORTANT THING
IS NOT HOW MANY
YEARS IN YOUR LIFE
BUT HOW MUCH LIFE
IN YOUR YEARS.

Edward Stieglitz

YOUR GRANDCHILDREN
HAPPILY POINT OUT
YOUR PHYSICAL
FLAWS WITHOUT EVEN
BATTING AN EYELID.

JUST ABOUT THE TIME A
WOMAN THINKS HER WORK
IS DONE, SHE BECOMES
A GRANDMOTHER.

Edward H. Dreschnack

WITH YOUR GRANDPARENTS YOU HAVE A FEELING THAT... YOU CAN DO ANYTHING, AND THEY WILL SUPPORT YOU.

Novak Djokovic

AS A CHILD I KNEW
ALMOST NOTHING,
NOTHING BEYOND WHAT
I HAD PICKED UP IN MY
GRANDMOTHER'S HOUSE.

V. S. Naipaul

YOU FEEL EXHAUSTED, RELIEVED AND RATHER WISTFUL ALL AT THE SAME TIME AS YOU WAVE GOODBYE TO YOUR FAMILY AT THE END OF A VISIT.

THE REASON GRANDPARENTS AND GRANDCHILDREN GET ALONG SO WELL IS THAT THEY HAVE A COMMON ENEMY.

Sam Levenson

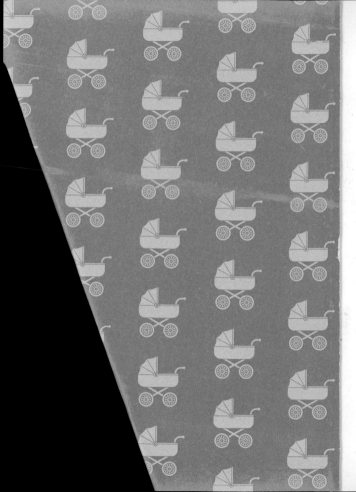

A REAL
FAMILY CONSISTS OF
THREE GENERATIONS.

Florence King

If you're interested in finding
out more about our books,
find us on Facebook at
SUMMERSDALE PUBLISHERS
and follow us on Twitter at
@SUMMERSDALE.

WWW.SUMMERSDALE.COM

A REAL
FAMILY CONSISTS OF
THREE GENERATIONS.

Florence King

If you're interested in finding
out more about our books,
find us on Facebook at
SUMMERSDALE PUBLISHERS
and follow us on Twitter at
@SUMMERSDALE.

WWW.SUMMERSDALE.COM